ALL YOU NEED TO KNOW

How to be a Sports Star

Contents

Have you got what it takes?	2
Pick a sport	4
Start training	6
Learn to love early mornings	8
Compete!	10
Make science your friend	12
Keep a training diary	14
Eat your way to the top	16
Plan your future	18
Snore your way to the top	20
Take an ice bath	22
The support team	24
Defeat 'the chimp'!	26
Coping with fame	28
Test yourself	30
Glossary	32
Index	32

Have you got what it takes?

OLYMPIC AND PARALYMPIC ATHLETES WANTED

YOUR COUNTRY NEEDS YOU!

Athletes are needed to go to the Games. For this demanding job you will need to:

- do lots of training and become very, VERY fit
- take part in competitions
- spend almost all your time working towards winning a medal.

In return, you will get to do the sport you love, travel the world and perhaps become a national hero.

Olympic and Paralympic athlete checklist

To become an Olympic or Paralympic athlete you will need to:

- ✓ train up to three times a day, six days a week – for the next six to ten years!
- ✓ suffer (for example by sitting in baths of icy water – see page 22)
- ✓ sleep for eight to ten hours each night
- ✓ spend nearly every weekend taking part in competitions
- ✓ eat three to four times as much food as other people
- ✓ do what you are told by your coach.

This book will help you with your training to become an Olympic or Paralympic athlete. It also offers tips on keeping healthy.

Pick a sport

Why stop at one?

Most people try lots of different sports before finding what they are best at. Few people are really, really good at more than one sport.

There are many track events at the Olympic and Paralympic Games. One of the longest distances to run is 10 000m.

Plenty of choice

There are 35 Olympic sports and 20 Paralympic sports to choose from, and each sport has lots of different **events**. All in all, there are hundreds of different competitions.

There are four different diving events at the Olympics.

Some athletes enjoy being part of a team. This is a basketball match at the **Paralympic Games**.

The rings is one of the many gymnastic events at the Olympic Games.

Name: Rebecca Romero
Born: 24th January 1980
Country: UK

Rebecca Romero is famous for winning Olympic medals at two different sports. Only one other woman has ever achieved this. In 2004 Rebecca won a silver medal for rowing and in 2008 she won a gold medal in the cycling.

Rebecca Romero only started cycling two years before she won her gold medal!

Start training

The race is on!

Once you find your best sport, there is no time to waste! It takes between six and ten years for an athlete to train for the Olympics or Paralympics.

Athletes have to train in all sorts of weather.

Join a club

Olympic and Paralympic athletes are usually members of a local sports club. They go to the club to train, get advice from coaches, and mix with other athletes.

Joining a club is a great way to make new friends too.

Sometimes you need others to encourage you to go training!

Find a club for your sport

You can find a local sports club through the sport's **governing body**. Sometimes people also find clubs through a local sports centre or by asking a friend.

Michael Phelps' nickname is the Baltimore Bullet.

Name: Michael Phelps
Born: 30th June 1985
Country: USA

Michael Phelps first joined North Baltimore Aquatic Club, when he was 7 years old. By age 10, he had set his first national record! Michael first went to the Olympics at the age of 15. At the 2004 Games, he won six gold medals. Then at the 2008 Beijing Olympics, Michael won EIGHT golds – more than any other person, ever.

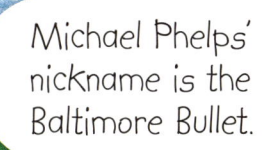

Learn to love early mornings

Early starts

If you like a lie-in, look away now! Most top athletes start their training long before anyone else is awake.

Top Tips

The best way to get up early is to put your alarm clock on the other side of the room. You'll have to get up to turn it off!

An early start means there will be no crowds at the training ground.

A busy day

After morning training, an athlete lets his or her body recover.

They don't get the rest of the day off, though!

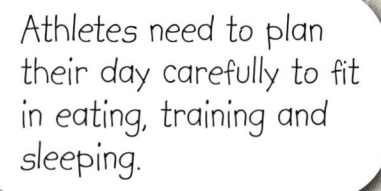

Athletes need to plan their day carefully to fit in eating, training and sleeping.

Diary of an Olympic Swimmer

5.15am	Snack: banana, hot drink. Cycle to the pool. Mustn't be late again!
6.00–8.00am	Morning training. Not too far to swim today — just 3.5 km.
8.15am	Breakfast: cereal, toast, boiled egg, juice. Relax for a couple of hours.
11.00am–12.30pm	Gym: upper arms, shoulders - goal = 40x2 push-ups.
1.00pm	Lunch: pasta, chicken, peas, yoghurt, fruit, water.
2.30–3.30pm	Sleep!
6.00–7.30pm	Evening training — swim another 3 km.
8.00pm	Dinner: fish curry.
9.00pm	Go to bed early — more to do tomorrow!

Compete!

Take part

Athletes don't get to the Olympics or Paralympics just by training. They also have to take part in competitions to prepare them for the biggest contest of all – the Games.

Inter-club meets are a good way to get used to competing.

Competitors must be of a certain standard before they can enter the national championships.

Inter-club meets

These are contests between clubs.
They are a great way to get competition experience.

County championships

To take part in the county championships, athletes have to reach a **qualifying standard**.

National championships

The best athletes in the country take part in these. The qualifying standard is even higher than for county championships.

10

Inter-country competitions

These are like inter-club meets – except athletes have to be the best in the country to get in the team!

Top Tips

For beating competition nerves:
- Do some relaxation exercises (see page 21).
- Watch the earlier races.
- Listen to music.
- Cheer your friends on.

European championships

Each country in Europe sends its best athletes to these.

World championships

World championships happen more often than the Olympics or Paralympics.

Olympic or Paralympic Games

The big one takes place every four years.

Only the best athletes will make it to the Games.

Make science your friend

New inventions

Scientists can improve the equipment athletes use. They have designed better shoes for distance runners, lighter bikes for cyclists, and special costumes for swimmers.

These costumes help swimmers so much that they are banned from competitions.

Name: Oscar Pistorius
Born: 22nd November 1986
Country: South Africa

Oscar Pistorius is a runner with a difference – his legs end below his knees. Despite this, he takes part in both Paralympic races and able-bodied races.

Oscar's lower legs had to be cut off when he was 11 months old, but this never stopped him. As a boy he played rugby, water polo and tennis. He went on to set world records for 100m, 200m and 400m running.

Oscar Pistorius has not let his lack of legs stop him becoming a top international runner.

Athlete testing

Science can help athletes learn how to improve their fitness. Equipment can be used to test how much an athlete's fitness is increasing.

Some inventions could give you an unfair advantage!

Measures how much oxygen is being used.

Measures how fast the athlete's heart is beating.

Checks skin and muscle temperature.

Computers can also check the athlete's diet by analysing his spit and wee.

This athlete is being tested in a sports laboratory.

Keep a training diary

Record it

A training diary is one of an athlete's most important training tools. Athletes write about how they train each day. They also make notes about what they do differently to prepare for a competition.

It is important for all athletes to build their strength.

Learn from it

Reading through their diary can give athletes important clues about which training routines help them to achieve their best results.

Ice skaters need to build their strength as well as their skating skills.

Top Tips

The key things to record are:
- your weight
- how fast your heart beats when you are resting
- whether your muscles are sore.

Don't let your training diary get in the way of training!

Training Diary of an Ice Skater

Monday 21st July
Weight: 71.5 kg
Heartbeat: 65 bpm
Morning: 30 minutes **weight training**. Rested for 1 minute after each set of weights.
Afternoon: Ice skating practice.
Evening: 15 minutes on the exercise bike, I cycled 8 km. Legs felt tired.

Ice skaters can record what went well about their performance and which parts of their training helped.

This really helped improve my fitness.

Tuesday 22nd July
Weight: 71.4 kg
Heartbeat: 67 bpm
Morning: 1 hour ballet class, swimming.
Afternoon: 20 minutes running, then weight training. Increased weight by 5 kg.
Evening: 45 minutes ice skating practice.

My muscles felt more relaxed when skating.

Eat your way to the top

Get it right

No one gets to the Games without eating the right food – and plenty of it! An Olympic or Paralympic athlete needs to eat three to four times as much as everyone else does.

Normal-sized meal

Big eaters

Most people need about 2000 **calories** a day. Athletes eat up to 8000 calories. It's actually quite hard work getting that much food inside you every day!

Olympic-sized meal

What's on the menu?

Like all of us, Olympic and Paralympic athletes need four types of food:

1 Carbohydrates, which provide energy for the muscles.

2 Proteins, which help an athlete's body grow and repair itself.

3 Fresh fruit and vegetables, which provide energy and the vitamins the body needs.

4 Fats and oils, which provide stored energy and help the body move freely.

Try it!

Athletes eat complex carbohydrates, such as brown rice, oatmeal or vegetables. These give out energy slowly, so the athletes can go longer without feeling hungry. See if these foods work for you too.

When do you normally feel hungry and want your lunch? Try eating porridge with chopped fruit and skimmed milk for breakfast. When do you feel hungry?

Plan your future

A long way to go

It's no good just getting a diary for six years' time and writing: go to the Games, win medal! Athletes (and their coaches) need to do a LOT more planning than that.

Olympic and Paralympic cycles

Olympic and Paralympic athletes plan their training in four-year periods, called cycles. They divide each cycle into four years. Finally, each year is divided up into smaller parts.

Month	Training
January to April	**Endurance** and skills
May to August	Increasing speed
September and October	Mixed competition and training
November	Less training
December	This year's big competition!

Planning your training will help you *be* ready for the big day.

Name: Tanni Grey-Thompson
Born: 26th July 1969
Country: UK

Tanni Grey-Thompson has been through more Paralympic cycles than almost any other athlete!

Tanni was 19 when she took part in the Paralympics for the first time, winning a bronze medal. This was just the start of her success. In total, Tanni took part in five different Paralympic Games and won an amazing ELEVEN gold medals!

Tanni Grey-Thompson celebrates winning the 800m wheelchair final at the 2000 Paralympic Games in Sydney.

Snore your way to the top

Early to bed

Grown-up athletes often need to go to bed by 9.00 pm. Younger athletes need even more sleep than that!

Age	Hours of sleep
3–5 years	12 hours
6–12 years	10 hours
Adult	8 hours

Children need much more sleep than adults.

Sleep can help you gain Olympic or Paralympic glory.

Why is sleep important?

Sleep helps the body to grow, recover from injuries, and get energy back. Athletes make their bodies work very, very hard, so they need more sleep than most people.

Going to bed early often isn't enough. Most athletes also have a nap in the afternoons!

Sleep helps injuries get better.

Try it!

To help you sleep, lie down, **tense up** your whole body and then slowly relax. Tense up your feet and toes, hold and relax. Tense up your hands and fingers, hold and relax. Tense up your shoulders, hold and relax. Feeling sleepy yet?

Take an ice bath

Cold comfort

Lots of top athletes take an ice bath after training. It can help their bodies recover more quickly.

Put your whole body in ice?

Athletes use ice baths in different ways, depending on their sport. Runners, for example, only put their bottom half in the cold water. Their top half stays dry and warm. Some even put on a thick coat while they are sitting in the bath!

This runner is taking an ice bath after a race.

Half fill the bath with cold water and tip in the ice.

The water is usually about 13 °C.

How long a bath?

Athletes stay in the ice bath for between 5 and 20 minutes, and then they have a warm shower.

Even colder

Some athletes go even colder. They use a **cryotherapy** chamber. Here temperatures go as low as -110 °C! If you stay in for more than three or four minutes, your eyeballs freeze!

In cryotherapy chambers people wear gloves and a mask to protect against frostbite.

The support team

A helping hand

Each top athlete needs a big support team to give them advice on their training and **tactics**. These people help athletes prepare for the big event, but they do not often go with them to the Olympics or Paralympics. **Spectators** usually see the athlete – not the whole team.

Coaches

Athletes work with one main coach. However, other coaches may give advice too.

Expert in sports medicine

They give advice on training to improve performance, weight and diet. Find out more on pages 14–15 and 16–17.

Ben Ainslie of Great Britain receives his gold medal for sailing at the 2008 Olympic Games in Beijing.

Without my team I would not be standing here.

Nutritionist

A nutritionist tells the athlete what to eat to get the best results.

Psychologist

A psychologist is an expert in how people think. This makes a big difference in sport – find out more on pages 26–27.

25

Defeat 'the chimp'!

What is 'the chimp?

Sometimes athletes begin to think they can't win a competition. When athletes think like this, they are less likely to win so they imagine these thoughts are being spoken by a real thing like a 'chimp'. They think of ways to defeat the chimp, like taping up its mouth or pushing it away! Then they are free to concentrate on the most important thing – winning!

British track cyclists learned how to defeat 'the chimp'. It helped them to win eight gold medals at the 2008 Beijing Olympics.

Don't let your chimp get in the way of winning!

Victoria Pendleton beat the chimp to become the Olympic champion at the 2008 Olympic Games in Beijing.

Try it!

To train your thoughts, firstly learn to recognise thoughts that stop you doing well. Then imagine these thoughts are coming from a chimp on your shoulder. The chimp is whispering the words, trying to put you off. Imagine taping the chimp's mouth shut. Now you can concentrate on what you need to do.

Coping with fame

The price of fame

The last thing an Olympic or Paralympic champion has to learn is how to cope with the fame. Many people they didn't know before will want to be their friend. They will be asked to give interviews and appear at awards ceremonies, and this takes up time. Champions still need lots of time for training if they want to win at the next Olympics or Paralympics.

You can't just relax when you've won the medal! People will want to talk to you. Here the British team are being interviewed at the Junior European Gymnastics Championships.

The support of fans can help an athlete succeed.

No one likes a big-head

A few famous athletes become big-headed. The fame makes them think they are better than other people, when really they are just better athletes.

Top Tips

To cope with fame:
- Remember you are only a better athlete, but not a better person than others.
- Think about the embarrassing things you have done as well as the great things.
- Do not let interviews (or TV and radio appearances) stop you from training.

Test yourself

Do you think you have what it takes? Do this quiz to find out!

1 You want to learn a new sport. Do you:
- **A** ask your friends if they do any sports?
- **B** try to teach yourself the new sport?
- **C** watch TV to get ideas?

2 You have a practice session at 8:00 a.m. on Sunday: Do you:
- **A** get up early and have a good breakfast?
- **B** get up just in time to make it?
- **C** forget to set your alarm and miss it?

3 Your have a big competition the next day. Do you:
- **A** do exercises to help you relax?
- **B** worry a little but get some sleep?
- **C** worry all night and not get any sleep?

4 Your coach tells you to do something. Do you:

A do what they say?
B listen and do some of what they say?
C pretend to listen but do your own thing?

5 You come first in a competition. Do you:

A feel happy but think about your next challenge?
B feel happy and give yourself some time to relax?
C tell everyone you are a winner and that you don't need to practise any more?

How did you do?

Mostly As
Congratulations! You definitely have what it takes.

Mostly Bs
Keep going. You are on the right track, but there is more you can do.

Mostly Cs
You have a lot of work to do. Don't forget, Olympic and Paralympic athletes never give up!

Glossary

analyse examine in detail

calories units used to count the amount of energy contained in food

cryotherapy treatment of injuries using cold, usually ice

endurance ability to do something for a long time

event a specially organised competition

governing body organisation that is in charge of a sport

Paralympic Games sporting event that follows the Olympic Games for athletes with disabilities

qualifying standard how good an athlete needs to be to enter the competition

spectator person who watches a game, race or performance

tactics plan for achieving an aim

tense up tighten

weight training lifting heavy objects to build strength

Index

calories 16
championships 10–11
chimp, defeating the 26–27
choosing a sport 4–5
clubs 6–7, 10
coaches 6, 18, 24
competition experience 10, 11
competition nerves 11
early starts 8
energy 17, 21
equipment 12
fame, coping with 28–29
famous athletes 5, 7, 12, 19
fitness 13
food 16–17, 25
ice baths 22–23
injuries 21
inter-club meets 10
nutritionists 25
planning 18
psychologists 25
sleep 20–21
sport science 12–13
sports medicine 13, 24
strength, building 14
support teams 24–25
team sports 5
thoughts, training 25, 26–27
training 6–9, 18
training cycles 18
training diary 14–15